Fables of the TIMES TABLES

written by...

pictures

Dennis Noble

Brigitte E. Kortright

Published by Yoga Pranayam Productions

Yoga Pranayam Productions
Published by Brigitte E. Kortright
32 Wheeler Avenue
Toronto, Ontario, Canada M4L 3V2

First published in Canada 1996
Copyright © Brigitte E. Kortright, 1996

Canadian Cataloguing in Publication Data

Kortright, Brigitte E. (Brigitte Elisabeth)
    Fables of the times tables

ISBN 0-9681339-0-8

1. Multiplication - Tables - Juvenile literature.

I. Noble, Dennis, 1940 -   II. Title

QA49.K67 1996   j513.2'13   C96-931856-1

Table of Contents

Dedicated
to
Robin, Jacki, Jasmin

and the other helpful gang:
Jim Ireland, Robert Kortright, Eric Parker,
Beth-Anne Cole, Shelley Frayer, and Emily French.

Foreword

For the sake of brevity and clarity mathematicians shortened long winded equations like 8+8+8+8+8+8+8 = 56 to 7 x 8 = 56 and organized the abbreviated equations into times tables. However, to memorize one hundred or more similar looking equations is still a challenge to most students. One way to manage the task is to repeat the equations over and over again until they are firmly embedded in the memory. This is called rote learning. The drawback of rote learning is that it is time consuming and extremely boring to most people.

Moreover, it has been proven that the mind stores facts and recalls them more efficiently when they have been made vivid and put into the framework of a story or rhyme. This is what this book is about. The numbers 0 to 11 have been given memorable characters, and the equations are events in their lives. To learn the times tables the student needs only to take in the illustrated stories and extract the pertinent knowledge from them. It appears to be a round about way to learn the equations, but in fact it makes for successful and accelerated learning as many workshops have proven.

In the 8 x, 7 x, and 6 x tables every equation is illustrated. That is not necessary for the lower times tables as by then the students have already learned many of the equations and repetition would be tedious. Consequently, the lower times tables have fewer illustrated equations. Instead they introduce additional learning skills.

The 5 x table teaches organization and alertness to patterns and details, the 4 x table teaches geometry and demonstrates the practical application of multiplication. The 3 x table illustrates resourcefulness and the application of memory aids when faced with the learning by heart of abstract data. The 2 x table is there for completeness and illustrates together with the 3 x, 5 x and 9 x table that students have different learning styles that are equally valid. The whole book encourages awareness and appreciation of alternative learning styles and individual expressions of intelligence.

To summarize, Fables of the Times Tables promotes a wholesome approach to learning. It draws mind, soul and body equally into the learning experience. Where the students otherwise would have encountered only a drab intellectual task, they experience with this approach a real joy in learning and an increase in self-esteem.

The Gang

Surely, you have heard about the magic of tears in fables. Well, so many tears of frustration have been shed over the barren bleak land of the times tables that at last the hard shell of the numbers washed thin, and their inner life peeked out and sprouted into a gang of flesh and blood. Take a close look at the opposite page and you will see that the number 8 is not just an eight, but also Little Eight, the youngest member of the roly-poly family, 7 is not just a seven but Hunter, who is so fond of shooting that his gun seems to be a permanent part of his body. 4 is four and Angular, who skips about on tap dance shoes and is Little Eight's best buddy. 9 is Egghead who loves math, statistics and computers; 5 is Willie Moneybags, the banker's son and 2, 3, and 6 are Horsie, Monkey and Snake, their animal friends.

O is Zero Zeronimus, the god of the numbers. Without him mathematics would be almost impossible, as the Romans found out. They didn't have a zero among their numbers. 1 is old Grandfather Fingerling, 10 is Grandfather Zen, the magician, and 11 is Grandfather with his pet, Eleven Eleven. Together they make up the venerated old people of the times tables gang. Their lives are so clear and simple, and their activities are so few they can be described in a few words. And if you want to learn their times tables, you can do it in seconds, while the others may take a couple of minutes. Let's therefore meet them first before we go and find out what is happening on Little Eight's birthday.

Willie Moneybags 5 5

Zero Zeronimus

Angular

Little Eight

Grandfather Zen

Monkey

Snake Hiss

Horsie

Eleven-Eleven

Egghead

Hunter

Grandfather Fingerling

Zero Zeronimus

Zero Zeronimus

Zero Zeronimus has two faces because he is a moody fellow. He is a grump, but a nice grump. On the one hand, he readily lends his friends his power rings with which they can increase their power by 10, 100, 1,000 etc., depending how many rings they borrow.

On the other hand, Zero Zeronimus hates to be drawn into multiplication all alone. Any number that wants to become big by directly multiplying with Zero loses out. Zero Zeronimus hurls their intent right back at them with an angry cry of "nought", and poof, all their expectations come to nothing.

Therefore, when you hear or see an equation with x 0 or 0 x, you know for sure, the result is always and without fail: 0. Even if the question is 7956963 x 0, the answer is still 0. Zero Zeronimus wins everytime.

7

Grandfather Fingerling

Grandfather Fingerling

Grandfather Fingerling's family tree goes all the way back to times when people first started to count on their fingers. He himself is very old. His body is so weak and slow that in additions he shuffles ahead only one step at a time.

When it comes to multiplication well, what do you expect? Not much happens. In his times table, the question always becomes the answer. Grandfather Fingerling reliably repeats what he has been asked. If you ask him, 4 x 1? his answer is 4, if you ask him 7 x 1? his answer is 7. And that is the total picture of Grandfather's multiplication life, except that he has an interesting hobby which is noticeable in the 10 x table and he has a pet, called Eleven Eleven.

11

Grandfather Zen

13

Grandfather Zen

In the 10 x table Grandfather Fingerling dresses up as a magician, borrows one of Zero Zeronimus' power rings and goes around as Grandfather Zen. It's his hobby. His trick is always the same. He throws the ring at the numbers that stand with him in the equation. For example, when 2 stands with him in the equation as in 2 x 10, then he throws the power ring and the answer becomes 20. When 3 stands with him in the equation, the answer is 30 and so on. It's a good show; Grandfather Zen certainly never tires of it, and it is almost as good as watching Grandfather walking around with his pet.

Now that's magic!

Eleven Eleven

Eleven Eleven

Grandfather Fingerling's pet is always found in the 11 x table. He is a big parrot. He always says what Grandfather says and as Grandfather, in his advanced old age, repeats the questions, his parrot repeats after him.

Listen to the echoes in the 11 x table! 8 x 11 = 88; 9 x 11 = 99.

But watch out for the last equation 10 x 11. Here Grandfather takes the stage and sends off his power ring with the old flick of the wrist and bingo, 10 x 11 becomes 110.

19

Little Eight

Little Eight's Birthday

Little Eight is the youngest of the Eights. The Eights are a roly-poly family. They are always happy, everywhere rounded and they love everybody, especially themselves.

Today, at one o'clock, Little Eight is rolling off the sofa, feeling warm and excited all over. It is his birthday, his friends are going to come and Grandfather promised him a magic show.

But what is this? What is swarming out of his clothes cupboard? Little Eight can't believe his eyes. His cat has freshly born kittens, a whole pride of them! Little Eight sits down in surprise and to coax them closer. There are eight of them. What shall he name them? He closes his eyes for a moment, imagines his birthday cake and names the kittens after the ice cream topping: Milk, Bean, Solid, Yolk, Gum, Glucose, Diglyceride and Choco.

I set of 8 = 8

Just then his older brother 2 x 8, bursts into the room. He is in such a hurry, he doesn't even see the kittens. "Sorry, kid brother," he shouts, "I'm going to miss your birthday cake. I'm taking Sweet 16 to bass horn practice, and afterwards there is a dance." Without waiting for a reply he dashes out.

Would he have seen the kittens, if there had been two sets of eight of them to make up his favourite number? *2 x 8 loves Sweet 16.*

2 sets of 8 = 16

As the door slams shut, the startled kittens run for cover.

Suddenly everybody is gone and Little Eight seems all alone. But he isn't. His first birthday guest has arrived. His friend Monkey sneaked in through the open window and now is silently tip-toeing at a snail's pace towards Little Eight to surprise him. Before he can reach him an ear splitting roar rocks the house. Monkey jumps several feet high and out of the window.

Little Eight hides under the table, his heart pounding. The door flies open and Horsie and Angular tumble in. They spy Little Eight under the table and linked together as a mischievous 24 they let out another very happy birthday roar. Little Eight pretends to be flattened out by the blast, then jumps up, hugs his friends and together they race up to the play room, shouting at the top of their voices, "3 x 8 = 24, a very happy birthday roar! 3 x 8 = 24, a very happy birthday roar!"

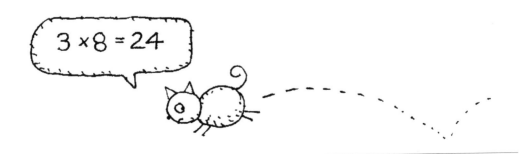

Little Eight's cookoo clock calls four times and the friends know that they have a whole hour for play before more guests will arrive. Angular cartwheels off to the toy chest and Little Eight rolls after. They rummage in the toy chest and there they find Monkey, still scared, and still trembling. He climbed back in through the attic window and hid in the toy chest. Horsie gently nudges him out of the box. Monkey looks sad. He is *dirty, too.*

Horsie gently nudges him out of the box and washes him clean.

At five o'clock Willie Money-bags and some aunts and cousins pop in. Throwing his arms wide open, Willie beams at Little Eight, "Happy Birthday!" "Many happy returns and what's for tea?"

Little Eight beams back at him. "What's for tea? Good question. Here it comes!" And he quickly whispers something into Angular's ear, they cross hands and he spins her around so fast, that his head seems to fly off. Only his perfectly round belly shows.

"That's for tea, you get it?" they both shout and then they laugh so hard, their whole figure of 40 starts to wobble. Willie pounces on them. "Enough of this charade, you little beasties," he yells in a mock European accent, "Off to the drawing room with you. Serve your starving guest tea! You hear, I don't want forty, I want tea!" And after a brief wrestling match Willie locks their heads under his arms and drags the laughing friends in the direction of the tea cozy.

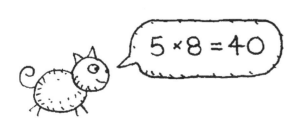

31

eanwhile Cousin Snake sits curled up on the sofa. You know about Snake. Her ancestors once lived in paradise, and she has match-making in her blood. She can't help noticing how well Angular and Little Eight get along. She sits there day dreaming. Her entire head is filled with one bright vision: she sees Angular and Little Eight married.

So, when Little Eight plunks himself down beside her on the sofa, Snake can't hold back any longer and excitedly whispers into his ear, "Angular is so hot, and you are so foxy. It's your fate to be Mrs. and Mr. 48!"

Little Eight's jaw drops and his face flushes crimson. He is totally embarrassed. "For goodness sake, Snakie, what are you thinking of?" he protests, "This is my birthday, not my wedding!"

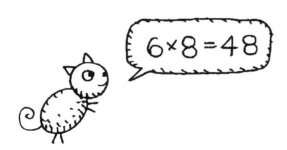

Luckily Hunter bursts into the room and saves Little Eight from his embarrassment. They all stare at him. What on earth is he bringing? Hunter swings his gift. "Happy birthday," he shouts across the room at Little Eight. "How are you? Let me uncoil your birthday present. It's 56, a wonderful snakie mix. I won it at my shooting competition. The snake is tame. Look, its holding out a fiver for you! I won it. But now it is yours," and he hands Little Eight five dollars and a mighty snake.

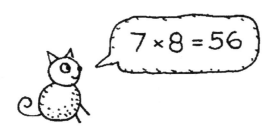

Wow, what a birthday. Little Eight is happy. He looks around and catches a glimpse of himself in the mirror. He admires his handsome roly-poly shape. Then Snakie's wedding prediction pops back into his mind. "Snake is crazy," he chuckles to himself, "I'll never be the right match for Angular. I don't have foxy eye lashes like her, three beauty spots and athletic shoulders. No!" And with a little sigh he concludes, "Too bad, but I'll never be a *sexy four.*"

gain the door bell rings. Little Eight rushes to the door. "It'll be my magic show," he yells as he is running. He flings the door open, and there stands Egghead, waving a present at him. She gives him a big grin and says, "Look what I have got for you: Definitely the most politically incorrect present. I looked it up in the statistic. Guess what it said? It said, parents are all up in arms about it, but little boys still like to play with toy guns and horses. Is that so?"

Little Eight grins as he pulls his present from the wrappings. "It sounds alright to me. It's just what I wanted: 72, a gun and a horse, all brand-new!"

39

At that moment Grandfather Zen enters and calls from the hall, "Little Eight! Eightie? Come, it's time for the cake and a magic show!"

When everyone is present, Grandfather waves his magic wand, spins his power ring, murmurs a spell and poof, the lights go out. When they come on again, Little Eight is changed to a radiant Eighty, crowned with a flaming birthday cake. There is instant applause and Grandfather Zen graciously bows to the cheering crowd.

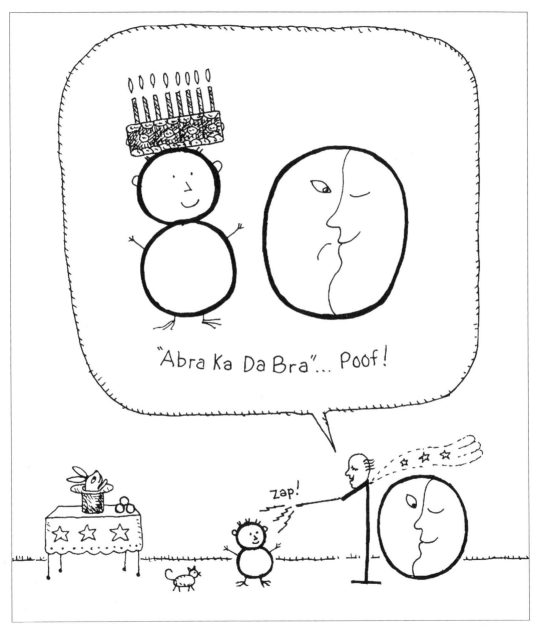

Summary

1 x 8 is 8, we know,
Little Eight is all a-glow.

2 x 8 loves sweet 16,
Wants to treat her like a queen.

3 x 8 equals 24,
A very happy birthday roar!

4 x 8 is 32,
A sad monkey, dirty, too!

5 x 8 asks, "What's for tea?"
"Watch the charade 'n you'll see!"

6 x 8 is cousin Snake,
Dreams of Mrs. 'n Mr. 48.

7 x 8 is 56,
Buddy Hunter's snaky mix.

8 x 8 a sexy four?
Little Eight doubts it more and more.

9 x 8 is 72,
A gun plus horse, all brand new.

10 x 8, a Grandpa's call:
"Oh, Eightie, come one, come all."

43

Hunter

Hunter's Shooting Competition

Hunter is such a good shot that he has been invited to a shooting competition. He will have to hit numbers that have fives and zeros in them. The person with the highest score will go on a safari. Hunter is so excited, he practices shooting all day, hardly taking any breaks for lunch and dinner.

His friends are appalled. "He wants what?" they cry out in disbelief, "He wants to win a Safari and shoot animals? He is on his way to become a trigger happy moron!" "No way," they promise each other, "We'll gang up on him and make him miss. It's for his own good!"

Meanwhile, at the 1 x 7 event, Grandfather Fingerling wishes Hunter luck. "Stay alert," he warns, "Some numbers will move more quickly, some could pop out, some may be objects."

Hunter thanks him, looks for the numbers and then fires only one shot. He ignores the fives and zeros and goes straight for number seven. "I know, I'll lose points," he says to himself, "but to start with, I must have seven. It's my lucky number. I'll catch up with the score later, that won't be a problem."

Hunter strides energetically toward the 2 x 7 event. He has to hit fifteen clay pigeons.

In the meantime, the anti-shooting gang can't decide who should make Hunter miss. They throw a coin. By the time Horsie comes up as the winner, Hunter is long gone. Horsie storms after him. He is almost too late. Hunter has shattered 14 of the 15 clay pigeons. He is aiming again. In a mad gallop Horsie brushes past him. Startled Hunter jerks the trigger and shoots the air. "Blasted Horse," he yells after Horsie, "Because of you, I shot 14!"

Horsie is ordered to stay home. Reassured, Hunter makes his way to the 3 x 7 event. His target is a pyramid of bottles. He takes careful aim. He has no idea that hidden in the trees, Monkey also takes aim and fires. Just as Hunter pulls the trigger, a rotten banana splashes against his forehead. Hunter misses totally.

Enraged Hunter swivels around, glares at the trees and in a fit of fury stomps the ground so hard that twenty-one bottles topple down. A loud speaker announces, "Hunter hit 21."

Stupefied Hunter turns around and stares at the bottles. Monkey slips away to tell everyone, "Hunter got 21."

For the 4 x 7 event the friends decide to be less obvious. Hunter may begin to suspect them. They therefore send Angular to be with Hunter. She goes equipped with a big bag of cherries and a teaspoon.

Hunter is glad to see her. Proudly he points to the rapidly revolving disk of numbers that he has to hit. He explains the rules to Angular but Angular is not interested. "Hang on, Hunter," she interrupts, "See that? There is 28; 28 is my lucky number." Angular is in a happy state. "It looks just like my buddies, Horsie and Little Eight. Let's see who can hit it first. You can use bullets and I will shoot cherry pits with my teaspoon." Hunter hits it right away, but then the blasted loudspeaker comes on again and announces, "Hunter hits 28. If you don't do better in the next event you'll be disqualified."

For the 5 x 7 event the friends decide to back off. Hunter wouldn't ever be the same if he lost altogether. This time they wish him luck. Willie Moneybags waves at him from the ranks because he has sponsored this event. The jackpot is a fast revolving silver cup with numbers printed on it. Hunter aims. With nobody to put him off, he promptly hits 35. He hits the jackpot, feels alive.

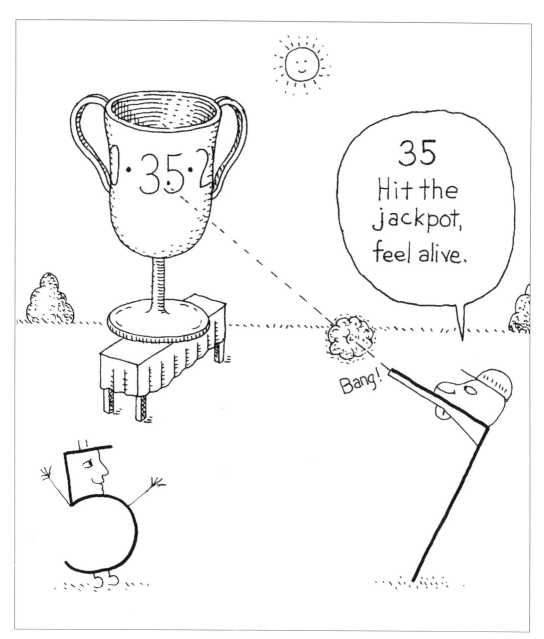

Happy, and with his head in the clouds, Hunter struts off to the 6 x 7 event. He spots a moving number tape on the far side of the pool. He doesn't see Snake waiting for him in the grass. He aims. Oops! He slips. He hits 42. Snake was under his shoe.

Hunter kicks off the mud. He still has a chance to be the best. The 7 x 7 event is coming up. Whoever hits 50 will get lots of money and plenty of bonus points. Hunter is confident because 7 x 7 contains two sevens and seven is his lucky number. He sees himself already strutting through a cheering crowd with a golden 50 on his lapel. He aims and fires. 49! He squares his chin to hide his disappointment but then throws himself headlong into the grass. "The lucky prize was almost mine," he moans.

Hunter still shakes with disappointment as he arrives at the 8 x 7 event. He has to shoot when two rotating disks combine to make fifty-five. Hunter's hand trembles just slightly and, "Oh, roly-poly fiddle-sticks," Hunter cries out, "I got 56! What is the matter with me? Fifty-five would have made me rich."

56 earns him a consolation prize: Five dollars and a big tame snake. The snake snatches the money, Hunter seizes the snake, and trots off to surprise Little Eight at his birthday party.

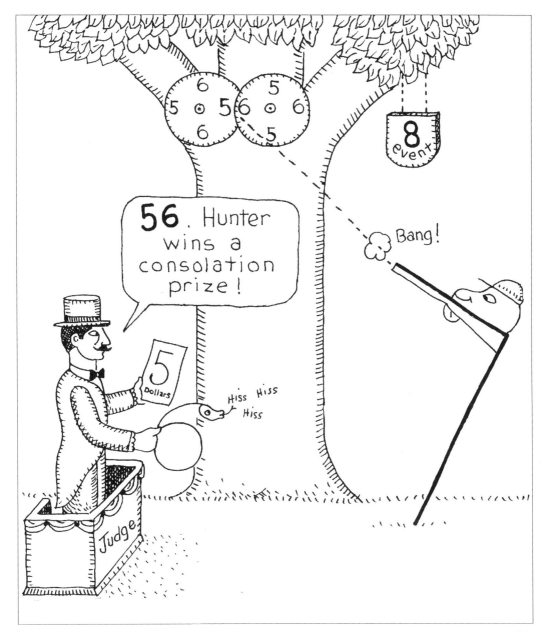

Egghead invites herself to the 9 x 7 event. She is fascinated by numbers. She calculates the relationship between the distance of the target and the weight and speed of the bullet. Then she excitedly explains to Hunter how her equations could improve his performance.

Hunter tries to follow her train of thought but gets all muddled in his head in the process. While he thinks about how to shoot, he makes the worst shot of his life. He hit 63. "Egghead distracted me."

Totally discouraged he throws his gun to the ground and hides his face in his sleeves. "Why can't I do it?" he sobs, "I don't want to go on a safari. I could never ever shoot an animal for fun, but I do love to shoot."

While Egghead quietly picks up his gun, she thinks ruefully, "We all misread Hunter." Aloud she says, "Come on, Hunter. Give it one more chance," and she gently puts his gun back under his arm.

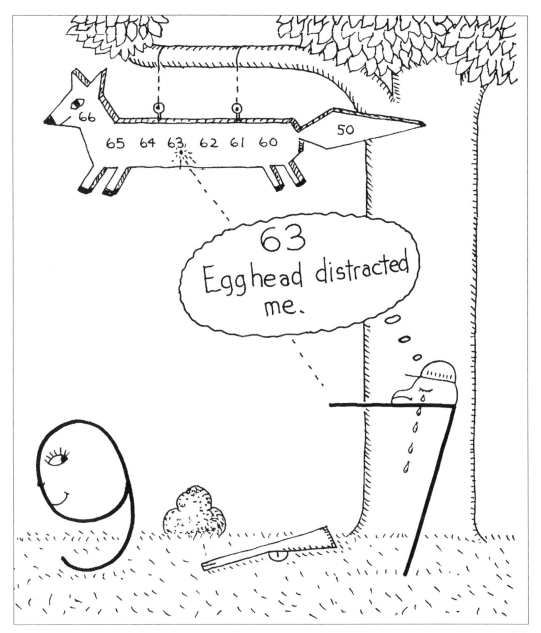

The whole gang including Grandfather Zen comes to see the important final event. This time Hunter has everyone's blessing, and Grandfather waves his magic wand just to make double sure.

Hunter's targets are 70 helium balloons rising towards the clouds. He blasts away and with every bang, he relaxes more and his face brightens. He gets all 70 before they drift out of reach. Gleefully he returns home and wonders whether relaxation was the key?

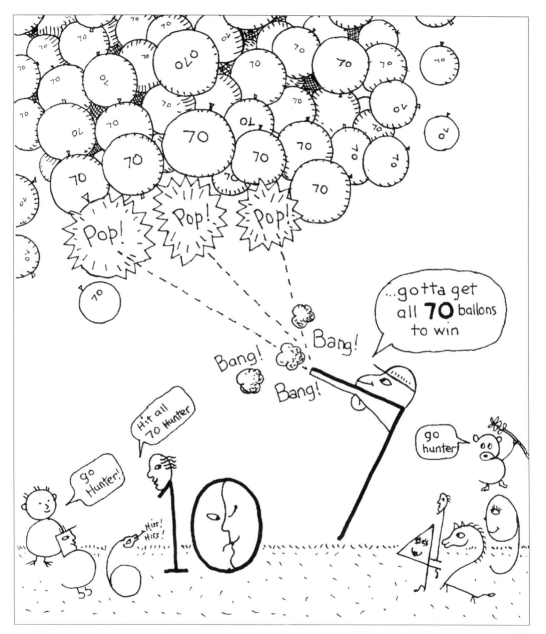

Summary

7, 14, 21 ...
so far no fun

4 x 7 ... 28 ...
Angular is in a happy state.

5 x 7 ... 35 ...
"Hit the jackpot! Feel alive!"

6 x 7 ... 42 ...
Snake got under my shoe.

7 x 7 ... 49 ...
The lucky prize was almost mine.

8 x 7 ... 56 ...
Roly-poly, fiddlesticks!

9 x 7 ... 63 ...
Egghead distracted me.

10 x 7 ... 70 ...
Relaxation is the key.

67

Snake

Hiss!

Hiss!

Hexagonia's Nightmare

Snake was out of pocket money, so she decided to earn some by teaching her times table. She put a note into the local community paper and sure enough three days later, a little kid called. She said her name was Hexagonia Slumberon, and she hadn't learned the 6 x table yet, because just looking at it would put her to sleep. Snake didn't believe her and asked her to come over.

Sure enough, there she is now with Snake at her first lesson, and looking at the times table, a sudden feeling of tiredness sweeps over her. Drowsily she reads, "1 x 6 = 6" and her eye lids start to droop.

71

Much like a heavy weight champion, Hexagonia struggles to keep the eyelids from drooping further. She manages just long enough to read out loud, "2 x 6 = 12". Then she lets go and they fall shut. That's it: Hexagonia is fast asleep. Only in a faint response to her last fleeting thought, her breath blows out in fits and starts like a receding steam engine, puffing, "Twelve ... twelve... twelve..."

Snake looks on, stumped. Then with a glint in her eye, she goes into action. "Aha," she says to herself, "The kid is bored. The kid wants a more interesting time. At your service, kiddo. Customer is king, as they say." And making herself very still, Snake begins to beam her thoughts at the slumbering kid, and sure enough, Hexagonia begins to dream.

In her dream, Hexagonia's nose rests deep in a wonderful soft, fluffy pillow. But suddenly the pillow hardens as if somebody is pumping it up like a bicycle tire. After three puffs, instead of hugging a pillow, Hexagonia is hugging a huge snake egg. The egg has '*eigh-teeny*' crack. The tiny crack widens and suddenly the shell caves in and Hexagonia's head plunges down into a tight ball of wriggly baby snakes. There are 18 of them, all madly hissing. Hexagonia screams and runs off in terror.

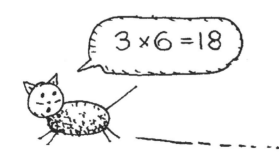

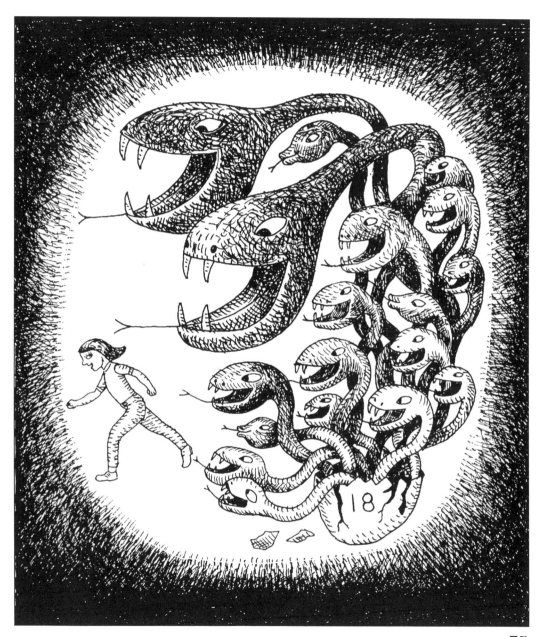

She blindly runs into the darkness and almost falls head over heels through an open trap door. She catches herself just in time and cautiously peers down into the opening of the dark, deep pit. She barely makes out the shape of 24 in the dim light. It's Horsie and Angular, trapped. But what are they doing? Mesmerized by a big black snake they are nervously dancing to the snake's menacing rattle, miserably crying out with every beat, "4 x 6 = 24 4 x 6 = 24 4 x 6 = 24." The sound of their voices alone is enough to make Hexagonia reach out with compassion. But barely has she lowered her arm to help, when the snake shoots up, ready to strike her face. Feverishly, Hexagonia jerks back and slams the trap door. "The whole place here is infested with snakes," she thinks, feeling her heart pounding. She looks around for a safe spot.

She sees a shimmering pool in the moonlight and beside it the still, stone statue of a monkey. Together they look like a huge 30 and a safe haven. Even if 5 x 6 = 30, and even if the water is dirty, I will escape. With one mighty determined leap, she dives in.

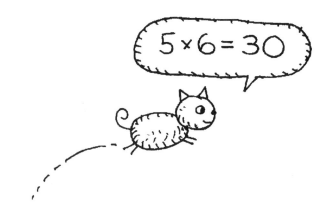

79

Relief. The water blocks all sound and Hexagonia relaxes, only to shrink back in terror. Something slimy slithers over her skin. The whole pond is teeming with water snakes. They are sliding up to her, hissing and spitting into her ear, "6 x 6 = 36 ... 6 x 6 = 36." One of them has a lisp.

Frantically she heads for shore and throws herself on the beach. She is just in time to see Hunter slip on a snake. "You, too?" she yells, "Watch out! There is a snake under your shoe. Help! I'm sinking, drowning in goo!" A calm voice replies, "Oh? And before you do, please remember 7 x 6 = 42." Hexagonia loses consciousness.

83

When she comes to, she is dangling from a fork. Greedy eyes examine her. She stares back in bewilderment. A thousand questions cram into her mind at once. But one thing is crystal clear to her. They are giants, and she has seen them before. She has never been face to face with any giant, but somehow these two look familiar. Who are they?

She swallows her fear and wriggles to take a closer look. They are Mrs. and Mr. 48! How did they get so big. There is no more time to think. She hears a shriek and the shocked cry, "Oh darling, a cockroach!" and a quick flick of Mrs. 48's wrist sets her flying through the air.

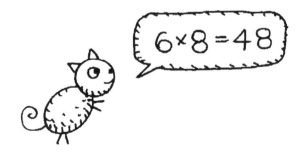

85

She lands with a thud on the very edge of the top step of a steeply winding staircase. She tumbles down, step by step, raising clouds of dust.

Egghead stand at the foot of the staircase, calmly watching Hexagonia's progress, counting and calling out for every tenth step on Hexagonia's spiralling path downward: "10... 20... 30... 40... 50...." When Hexagonia has only a few steps to go, Egghead speeds up to call out the last 4 steps. Then she sums it up: "That's 54 altogether. 54? The kid must be sore. You did well to soften her fall, or she would have 9 x 6 = 54 forever printed on her backside in blue and green."

Bewildered Hexagonia raises her head to see who Egghead is talking to, and with a shocked groan she blacks out again. The door mat she had landed on is not a doormat at all but another huge ghastly snake.

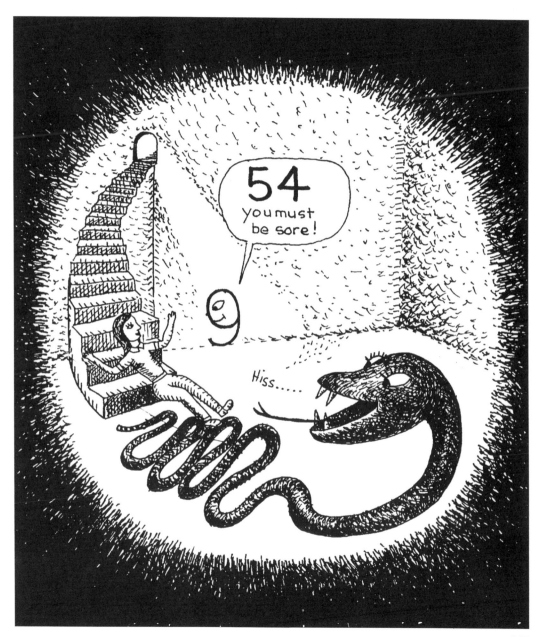

When she recovers, bright sunshine warms her skin. She lies with her nose deeply buried in soft green grass. Grandfather Zen stands beside her. "He is going to tell me that 10 x 6 = 60," she thinks. But he, grinning broadly, asks, "Would you like a summary?"

No!" With that agonized scream of hers, Hexagonia sits up with a jerk. Fully alert, but still pale from the terror of the nightmare, she looks around. She is back at the desk in her tutor's room. Snake is sitting beside her. "No summary?" Snakes asks her, barely hiding a mischievous smile.

"No summary. No thank you!" There is no doubt in Hexagonia's mind about that. And still shaking in her boots, she adds, "But thank you, Snake, I'm not likely to forget your lesson!"

Willie Moneybags

Willie Moneybags, The Richmeister

Willie Moneybags is the rich kid with the striped shirt and the combat boots. His father is a banker and Willie has learned his father's trade. When other kids ask him, "Hey, Willie, how did you get so rich?" he always responds, "Come to my afternoon class, I'll show you. In the meantime save your nickels, they will come in handy. It's rule number one: If you want to become rich, collect money! And remember, time is money. To read clock faces, you'll need to know your 5 x table. So, be prepared, we 'll practice that times table, too."

In the afternoons Willie indeed gives lessons on how to become rich, and he starts each one with physical fitness. He explains, "See, I've already told you, if you want to be rich, you can't waste time. Pack it in. Get the blood going. Practice the 5 x table at the same time. Here we go! 5 jumping jacks to warm up!"

I started off with a nickel and look where it got me.
5¢ one nickle
Willies piggy BANK

Now, for 1 x 5, raise one arm and fist, bring them overhead and back! Equals five! Thrust your arm forward, spread those fingers wide. Good.

2 x 5, make two fists, both arms go overhead and back! Equals ten! Both arms come forward, spread your fingers wide!

10 more jumping jacks! Now down into squatting, and begin Russian dancing. Kick those heels out from underneath you." Everyone topples over on their backs and that is just as Willie had planned it.

"Continue the 5 x table!" he yells. "3 x 5, two fists plus one foot point to the ceiling. Expand! Lower your outstretched arms and leg half way! Equals fifteen! Bring your outstretched arms and leg together, spread the fingers and the toes of that airborne foot!

4 x 5, lift both arms and legs to the ceiling. Keep them outstretched and lower them half way! Equals twenty! Bring them together, and lift your head to admire your fully outstretched hands and toes. Now draw your knees towards your chest and rock twenty times back and forth, chin to the chest, and then jump up and continue with juggling. Watch my demonstration!"

Zzzzz ----

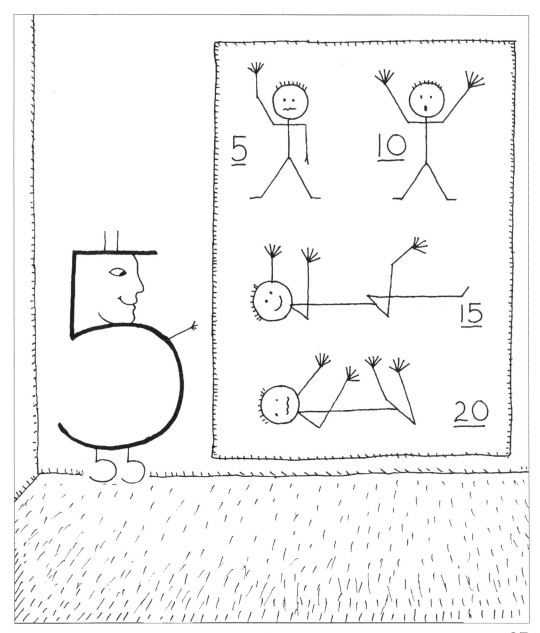

Willie pulls 5 nickels from his pockets, shows them to the class and then juggles them, round and round, and faster and faster. Finally he catches them all in one hand, and when he opens it, only one quarter, one 25 cent coin shines in his palm.

Before the puzzled faces of his class, Willie repeats his magic 5 x 5 = 25 trick. Then he encourages everyone to either try this juggling act or to do 25 push-ups. "It's good to feel your times table in your muscles." Willie grins and does 25 push-ups himself. At last everyone is allowed to relax.

The relaxation is the best part of the whole lesson, but Willie has no mercy and after five minutes he calls everyone back to attention.

"Now, if you had come only to learn the 5 x table by heart, you could almost go home now," Willie explains to the class, "Because the only equation you don't know is 9 x 5. The others you know already from Little Eight, Hunter, Snake and the Grandfathers. However, since you came to find out how to become rich, you don't have much of a choice, you must practice rule number two which is: If you want to become rich you have to do the customary plus a little bit more. So, in this case, what is this little bit more?"

For one, you have to count money, and count it fast. Willie dumps a bucketful of nickels on the table. "Count it," he commands. The room buzzes, "5, 10, 15, 20, 25, 30, 35, 40, 45, 50, 55..."

When the results come in, Willie asks, "But how are you sure you counted right?" Everybody begins to count again and again the room buzzes, "5, 10, 15, 20, 25, 30, 35..." Willie waves his arms and yells like a sergeant major to make himself heard above the noise. "Hold it," he yells, "Time is money. Tell me with *one* glance whether your answer is right or wrong?" No response from the class. Willie puts a poster on the wall. "This familiar shape of the five

points on the dice may give you an idea. If you place your coins in such a pattern, then you can check in seconds whether you counted right."

When everyone has also learned to count a big pile of nickels, quarters and pennies with certainty, Willie calls for a pause and proclaims, "Good! Now you can appreciate rule number three: If you want to become rich, you must train yourself to see patterns. You learn much faster that way and you can react quicker. However, this rule is only good if you also train yourself to try things in more than one way. That's rule number four. I'll give you another example where both these rules apply. Look at this 5 x table."

101

Willie hangs up a poster of the 5 x table (fig.1).

"Doesn't almost everyone learn it just like this? You start at 1 x 5 = 5 and you work your way down to 10 x 5 = 50.

Now, that's how most people do it. But it's not the best way, because you don't make use of the pattern that is hidden in the 5 x table to help you learn it.

I learn the 5 x table differently. I make two blocks out of the 5 x table, just like this (fig. 2). I group all the even factors in one block and all the uneven factors in the second block. Why do I do it like that? Because it reveals the pattern. Now you can take in the pattern in an instant.

Let's look at the block with the even factors. Notice that every one of the products to the right side of the equal sign ends in 0.

Look at the second block that has the uneven factors. All its products end in 5.

You can also notice that the tens in the product or answer are half of the sum of the question. Let's look closely at 8 x 5. Half of eight is 4. So the answer to 8 x 5 is therefore 40. Do you want to know how much 6 x 5 is? Easy. Half of six is 3, so the answer to that question is 30.

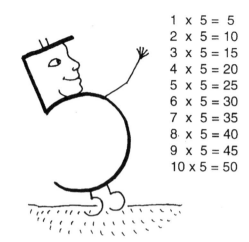

```
 1 x 5 =  5
 2 x 5 = 10
 3 x 5 = 15
 4 x 5 = 20
 5 x 5 = 25
 6 x 5 = 30
 7 x 5 = 35
 8 x 5 = 40
 9 x 5 = 45
10 x 5 = 50
```

Fig 1

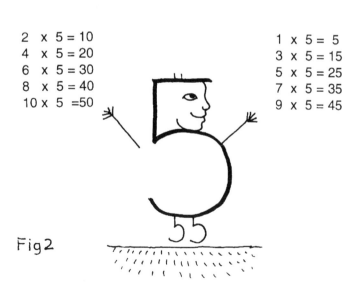

```
 2 x 5 = 10        1 x 5 =  5
 4 x 5 = 20        3 x 5 = 15
 6 x 5 = 30        5 x 5 = 25
 8 x 5 = 40        7 x 5 = 35
10 x 5 = 50        9 x 5 = 45
```

Fig 2

Now, lets go back to 9 x 5. Of course, by now you know the answer, because half of 9 is 4.5, and so the answer to 9 x 5 must be 45. But there is another way to memorize it. It helps, if you have an eye for detail. Take Egghead. She is quick to see my combat boots and that will trigger in her mind the fact that Angular has tap dance shoes. So, when Egghead looks at me, as in 9 x 5, she never sees me alone, but sees Angular and me, dancing together in 45, beating out the rhythm with our shoes."

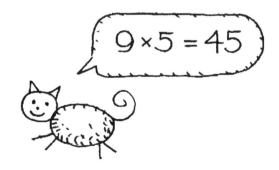

Other people see other patterns. When Angular looks at me in 4 x 5, she doesn't really see me, she sees only my sports car: horse power. Do you see the empowered horse, horse power in 20? But we're getting sidetracked. Let's learn rule number five: If you want to become rich, work on what you're good at. Know what you know and apply it. Take Hunter for a model. 7 x 5 = 35: Get rich by shooting all the jackpots in the country, if that is, what you love to do.

107

Let's sum it up.

If you want to become rich:

1) Collect money

2) Work a bit harder than the average

3) Don't waste time. See the patterns!

4) Be bold! Try things more than one way.

5) Work on what you're good at; and last but not least:

6) Earn a commission by signing up all your friends and relations for this course.*

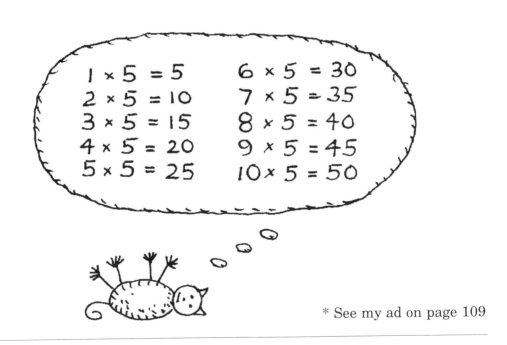

$$1 \times 5 = 5 \qquad 6 \times 5 = 30$$
$$2 \times 5 = 10 \qquad 7 \times 5 = 35$$
$$3 \times 5 = 15 \qquad 8 \times 5 = 40$$
$$4 \times 5 = 20 \qquad 9 \times 5 = 45$$
$$5 \times 5 = 25 \qquad 10 \times 5 = 50$$

* See my ad on page 109

MONEY A PROBLEM ?
NO PROBLEM!
call Willie Moneybags
THE RICH MEISTER
Tel. 555 5555 or   555 2045

Angular

Angular's Delicious Answer

Angular has long eye lashes, three beauty spots and tap dance shoes. She loves to skip, hop, and dance. However, today she muses over her diary. She ticks off all the events of her times table that are known to every one. She hesitates at 4 x 4. "That's me looking in the mirror," she thinks and looks up into the real mirror. At once she makes a face; she doesn't like what she sees. "I'm all angles," she moans, "And my shoulders stick out a mile. When I grow up, I want to look like Sweet 16. That's what that equation is all about."

She is about to turn the page, when Little Eight bounces into the room. "I need help, Angie, with a math problem," he blurts out. Angular laughs. "You got the wrong person. Egghead is a better bet on that score. Math is her hobby." Little Eight persists, "No, no! I think you know this one. It has to do with you. I dozed off in multiplication class and now I don't know what four squared means. Do you?" "Oh yes, I do. Would you like a delicious answer?" Puzzled by this reply, Little Eight doesn't know what to say, except that food is always welcome. "Alright," Angular stuffs money into her pocket, "Let's go and shop."

Together they race to the store and Angular buys cherries, Smarties, and licorice. At home Angular pushes up her sleeves and says, "Let's start." Little Eight has no idea what all this has to do with 4 squared but he is willing to do anything for Smarties and cherries. "What can I do?" he asks.

"Let's place four cherries horizontally in a line with even spaces. Let's take more cherries and complete a vertical row of four downwards. Let's fill in the other rows. Well, what have we got?"

"A square. Four squared! This is cool." Little Eight studies the grouped cherries. "So 4^2 actually means 4 x 4, but its called four squared, because in the real world you actually get a square if you arrange them this way. Do you know, I always learn math formulas by heart without thinking about them. I had no idea they made sense in the real world. Can I gobble up the answer?" "Wait," Angular seizes Little Eight's arm. "Tell me first, without counting, how many cherries are in 4 squared? Quick, tell me now." "16!" Angular lets go of Little Eight. "Right, they're all yours."

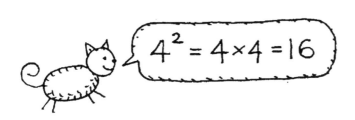

$$4^2 = 4 \times 4 = 16$$

After a while Little Eight asks, "What did you buy the Smarties for?"

"I was going to put down 3 x 4 = 12 and make you find out that it is a rectangle, and then have you arrange 5 x 4 = 20, etc. Eventually I was planning to show you that each times table has only one square. You escaped all that overkill by getting to the question directly."

"Oh, let's play anyway, Angie. You have to put the Smarties to good use," says Little Eight with his eyes on the candies. Angular shrugs her shoulders. "Okay, I'll put down the outer edges, and then you tell me the total number of Smarties before I put them down. If you don't get it right, I'll get the Smarties." Angular puts down 2 Smarties horizontally and 4 vertically. "8! That's too easy, Angie," Little Eight cries, "I hardly got any Smarties. Let's play big numbers."

They play until all the Smarties are gone. Then Angular gets the licorice out and places 4 pieces horizontally, and 6 vertically. Little Eight knows the answer to 4 x 6 very well, but he deliberately guesses wrong. He hates licorice. He leaves the licorice to Angular and eats the rest of the cherries.

117

Fully satiated they take a break and Little Eight asks, "What were you doing before I interrupted you?"

"I was crossing off all the publicly known events of my times table. Now, after our game, I can close the book, because everyone knows the answers." Little Eight wants to see it anyway. He opens the book randomly.

"What's this? 9 x 4 = 36 looks like a sad story. What happened?"

"Oh, it was a crazy afternoon," Angular explains, "Egghead had invited me over. Monkey and Snake wanted to come along. They had got it into their heads that Egghead would serve them fudge and straw-berry cream cake. But Egghead remembers only food for thoughts. So, when we arrived, there were only hulled strawberry stems to eat. Monkey and Snake were so upset they cried all afternoon because they had only 36 sticks for tea."

Little Eight all of a sudden sits up straight and asks, "Angie, have you seen Monkey today? He didn't come home yesterday, and I didn't see him today. Have you seen him?"

"No," Angular answers, "I haven't seen him either. That's not like him. Where could he be?"

Angular and Little Eight look at each other and burst out at the same time, "I'll bet you, when we find him, he'll be sad and *dirty, too!*"

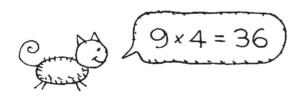

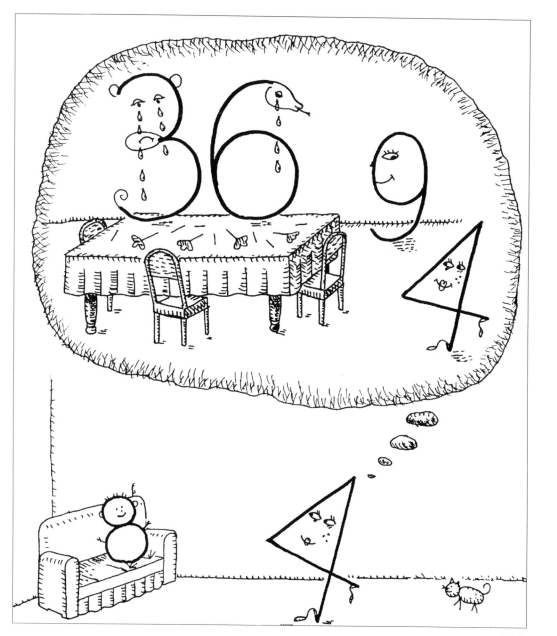

119

Monkey

Monkey's Bad Day

Monkey's playful days in the rain forest came to a sudden end. Hunters caught him and brought him to the city. Scientists, eager to test his brain, sat him down in a bleak lab and told him to learn the 3 x table.

Monkey threw his head back and screamed for hours. He was too scared and too homesick to even see the times table, let alone learn it. Instead of numbers he saw only black scratches on white paper. However, he saw the door of the lab very clearly. One day, when he saw his chance, he escaped and hid in Little Eight's attic. He made friends with Little Eight and the whole gang. He totally forgot the lab until he was recaptured and put back in front of the 3 x table. "Learn the 3 x table or there will be no food," they told him.

123

1 x 3 = 3

Miserable and frustrated, Monkey whimpers softly. How is he going to learn the times table? He has no idea, but he is willing to try. He is already hungry.

Diffidently he stretches out 3 fingers in order to remember that 1 x 3 = 3. That's easy enough. He leaves his 3 fingers fanned out in front of him to remind himself.

2 x 3 = 6

Then he turns to 2 x 3 = 6. Monkey spreads out three more fingers from the other hand. He looks down at his two hands for awhile to imprint the answer 6 firmly in his memory.

$3 \times 3 = 9$

Monkey adds three toes to his six outstretched fingers. Then he carefully counts all his extended digits. Yes, they do add up to nine. "But what if I run out of fingers and toes?" he suddenly panics, "what will I do then." "Oh," he groans, "I wish I was Egghead. She simply looks at the equations and remembers them without even trying."

That thought has given Monkey an idea. He thoughtfully stares at the equations. Then he thinks aloud, "3 x 3. 3 is me, Monkey. 3 x 3 = 9 is me looking at myself and wishing I was Egghead. Egghead is the nine." His whole face brightens up, but he doesn't dare to lift his fingers yet, as he glances at the next equation to test his new found learning strategy.

4 x 3 = 12

Again he thinks aloud, "4 is Angular, 3 is me, Monkey. What are we doing? We are fighting puff adders. They rear themselves and huff and puff poisonous gases in our faces going, "Twelve, twelve," with each strike. But we aren't scared. We shoot cherry pits into their open throats and that'll stop them.

5 x 3 = 15

That's Willie Moneybags and me, admiring my Queen. She is Queen Fifteen, and stands right in the middle of my times table.

Wow, I am already half way through, only five more equations to learn, then I can have breakfast!

Twang!

1 × 3 = 3
2 × 3 = 6
3 × 3 = 8
4 × 3 = 12
5
6   18
7 × 3
8 × 3 = 24
9 × 3 = 27
10 × 3 = 30

6 x 3 = 18

Halloween time! That's Snake and me. Snake watching, while I, Monkey, the mighty King Kong, hold 'eighteeny' Grandfather Fingerling and Little Eight in the palm of my paw shouting, "Trick or Treat?"

7 x 3 = 21

Here you can watch me, Monkey, the sure-handed, aiming a well directed banana. I can already see this rotten banana splashing against Hunter's forehead. With the muck in his eyes Hunter won't see the end of his gun and shoot 21!

Horsie

Horsie's Busy Day

Horsie loves to jump and run for fun. He rarely ever stops. While he is jumping and running, he sings his times table rhyme. It's not very poetic but he says it's fine. The singing is the important part:

Ho-Ho for a horse and you!

1 x 2 is 2, and good for you.

2 x 2 is 4, four knocks at the door.

3 x 2 is 6, six cubes of sugar for my morning fix.

4 x 2 is 8, eight cherries on a silver plate, served by Angular at a golden gate.

5 x 2 is 10, ten rich men, and Willie Moneybags with with a diamond pen.

Ho-ho for a horse and me, Naw Neh Noo Nah Nee!

6 x 2 is 12, twelve apples on my shelf.

7 x 2 is 14, fourteen beans in a soup tureen.

8 x 2 loves Sweet 16, the prettiest girl you've ever seen.

9 x 2 is 18, eighteen buttered toasts with margarine.

10 x 2 is 20, whoa, I've sung plenty.

But then Horsie takes another round and starts all over again...

Ho-Ho for a horse and you!

1 x 2 is 2, and good for you!

Egghead

Egghead Keeps Cool

Egghead is the smartest kid on the block, but in the eyes of some kids, she has weird taste. She loves patterns, encyclopaedias, and math. She spends almost all her free time in front of computers.

Today, just as she switches on her personal computer, she catches her reflection on the computer screen. She sees an excited egghead who just can't wait to find out all the things a computer can do.

"Now I know why 9 x 9 = 81," she thinks, "9 x 9 is me, reflected in the computer, and the answer is 81, because 81 rhymes best with computer fun. Computer fun is the very essence of me, Egghead."

In the meantime Horsie comes galloping through Egghead's backyard, ready to jump over her times table. At the very last moment he stops himself short and looks at the thing closely. Surprised he snorts, "Look, isn't it weird, 9 x 9 = 81 and 2 x 9 = 18. The answer is reversed. I wonder why that is so?"

The gang crowds around him to have a better look. Horsie hardly notices them, he is so deep in thought. Suddenly, a ripple of excitement run over his hide, as he announces to himself, "I think I know. Egghead lives for computer fun; she sits in front of the computer almost all day. I wouldn't last one minute in front of a computer. I love to jump and run all day and enjoy the sunshine. I am just the opposite of Egghead. That is why the product of these two equations is reversed, 18 is the reverse of 81, computer fun."

This statement of Horsie's causes an uproar among his friends. Everyone now notices that they are the opposite to somebody else in Egghead's times table. Hunter swivels around so fast, he almost knocks Angular down with his gun. "Why are the answers reversed in 7 x 9 = 63 and 4 x 9 = 36?" he asks her excitedly.

Monkey cries, "I know why the answer to 8 x 9 = 72 and 3 x 9 = 27 is reversed. It creates a link between my equations and Little Eight's. And so it should. We are buddies!" Even Snake raises her voice. Everyone talks at the same time and looks to Horsie for an explanation. Horsie can't cope. "Let me out of here," he groans and jumps over the fence without further notice.

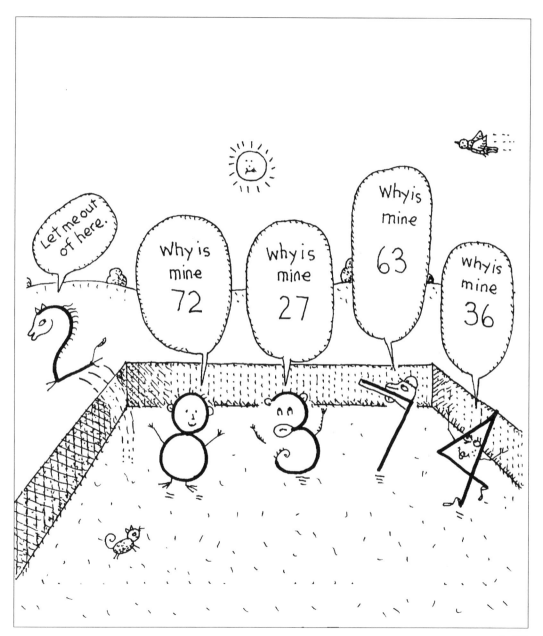

In the commotion somebody pushes Egghead's times table over and the numbers scatter all over the floor. "Oh, my!", "Oh, no!", "Oh, dear!" everyone gasps. Only Egghead keeps cool, and calmly examines the mess on the floor. Then she turns to Hunter who stands right next to her, and says, "I bet I can put my times table together faster than you can load your gun." Hunter is impressed. "I can load my gun in thirty seconds." "I think I need less time than that," retorts Egghead. "Let's see. Let's get Willie to time me."

Willie agrees and pulls a stopwatch out of his pocket. "Ready! Go!" he commands.

Egghead quickly picks up the numbers 0 to 9 to put the product of her times table together. She places them as fast as lightening in a neat column, muttering as she lays them down. "0,1,2,3,4,5,6,7,8,9, done! That's the tens column of the answers."

Then she rakes another lot of numbers together and places them in a neat column to the right of the tens. This time she starts at the bottom and works her way up. Again, she mutters as she works, "0,1,2,3,4,5,6,7,8,9. That's the unit column of the answers. Almost finished. Now to the question part of the equations," she says, as she wipes her brow.

All I have to do now is to pick up the questions and place them before the right answers. This time I'll start at the top with 1 x 9."

While she talks, she loses no time. When she places the last number down, Willie pushes the button of his stopwatch again and announces, "Twenty-nine seconds!"

Egghead holds out her hand and says, "Gi' me nine!" Willie grins and raises his hand, "Take five", he says. "By the way," Egghead adds, "you can check the answers in my table very easily. The sum of the tens and units in the product always adds up to nine." And a bit sheepishly she adds, "How is that for a bit of math trivia?"

151

All this time, Monkey has watched her open-mouthed. Suddenly Egghead turns to him and says, "Monkey, you are going to learn my times table." Monkey swallows hard. All the blood drains from his face. He pales visibly under his fur. He doesn't say a word, but his body language screams, "No! No! No!"

Egghead hears him alright, "Oh, don't worry," she tells him, "You'll be alright. I know, you think, you haven't got the brains, but let me tell you, you have the most intelligent fingers I have ever seen. Come, I'll show you a trick, I'll show you how to learn it with your fingers."

"Fan out all your fingers on the floor. That's it. Now, let's say, I ask you 4 x 9. You would simply tuck in four fingers for the 4 x. Now count your outstretched fingers. How many have you left?"

Monkey counts, "Six". "Right. Now you remember 6, because it is the unit part of the answer." Just to make sure, that he will remember it, Monkey writes down 6 with his foot. This time Egghead watches open mouthed. "Gosh, I wish I could do that," she sighs.

"Alright, for the second part of the answer you always stretch out one more finger. Then you count the thick knuckles of the tucked under fingers. That's the tens of your answer. How many tucked under finger have you got? Monkey counts, "Three". "Good. There you are. Put the 3 in front of the 6, and you have your answer to 4 x 9. It's 36."

"Let's play it again. Let's try 3 x 9."

Egghead and Monkey play for quite some time and each time Monkey speeds up. Soon he can place his fingers faster than Egghead. Then an amazing thing happens. Monkey doesn't need to use his fingers any more. The answer just pops into his head, as soon as the question is asked. Totally pleased, Monkey wriggles his toes and gazes thoughtfully down at his fingers. "I didn't know I had brains in my fingers," he murmurs to himself.

Monkey is so entirely lost in thought that he doesn't notice that the whole times table gang is crowding around him. Angular finally nudges him. "Let's go and party," she urges. They neatly put their times table into the closet and stroll into the kitchen to see what they can *divide* among themselves.